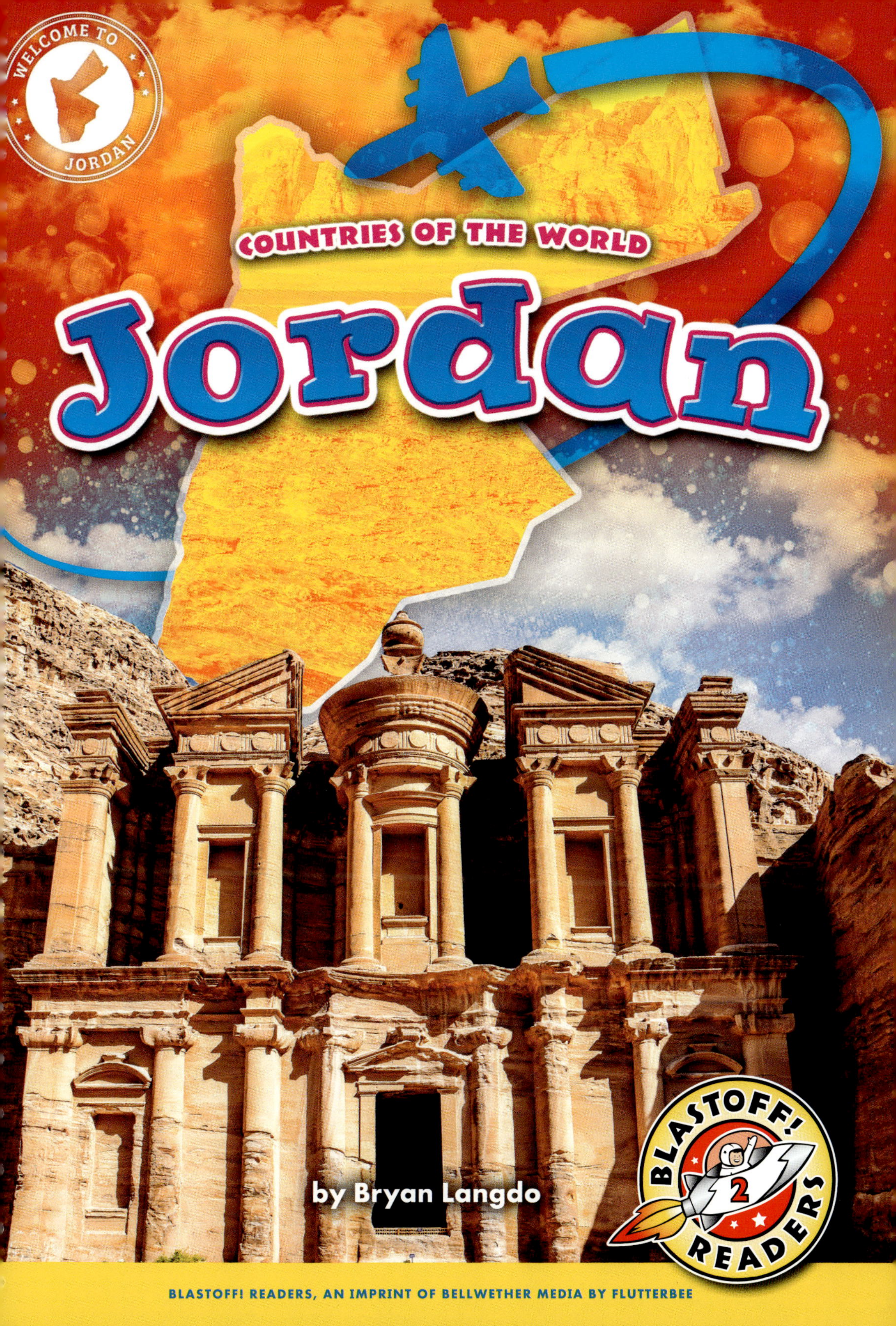
WELCOME TO
JORDAN
COUNTRIES OF THE WORLD
Jordan
by Bryan Langdo
BLASTOFF!
2
READERS
BLASTOFF! READERS, AN IMPRINT OF BELLWETHER MEDIA BY FLUTTERBEE

Blastoff! Readers are carefully developed by literacy experts to build reading stamina and move students toward fluency by combining standards-based content with developmentally appropriate text.

Level 1 provides the most support through repetition of high-frequency words, light text, predictable sentence patterns, and strong visual support.

Level 2 offers early readers a bit more challenge through varied sentences, increased text load, and text-supportive special features.

Level 3 advances early-fluent readers toward fluency through increased text load, less reliance on photos, advancing concepts, longer sentences, and more complex special features.

★ **Blastoff! Universe**

Reading Level

Grade K

Grades 1–3

Grade 4

This edition first published in 2026 by Bellwether Media, Inc.

For information regarding permission, write to Bellwether Media, Inc., Attention: Permissions Department, 3500 American Blvd W, Suite 150, Bloomington, MN 55431.

Library of Congress Cataloging-in-Publication Data is available at www.loc.gov or upon request from the publisher.

ISBN: 9798893047851 (hardcover)
ISBN: 9798893048858 (ebook)

Editor: Rachael Barnes Designer: Brittany McIntosh

Printed in the United States of America, North Mankato, MN.

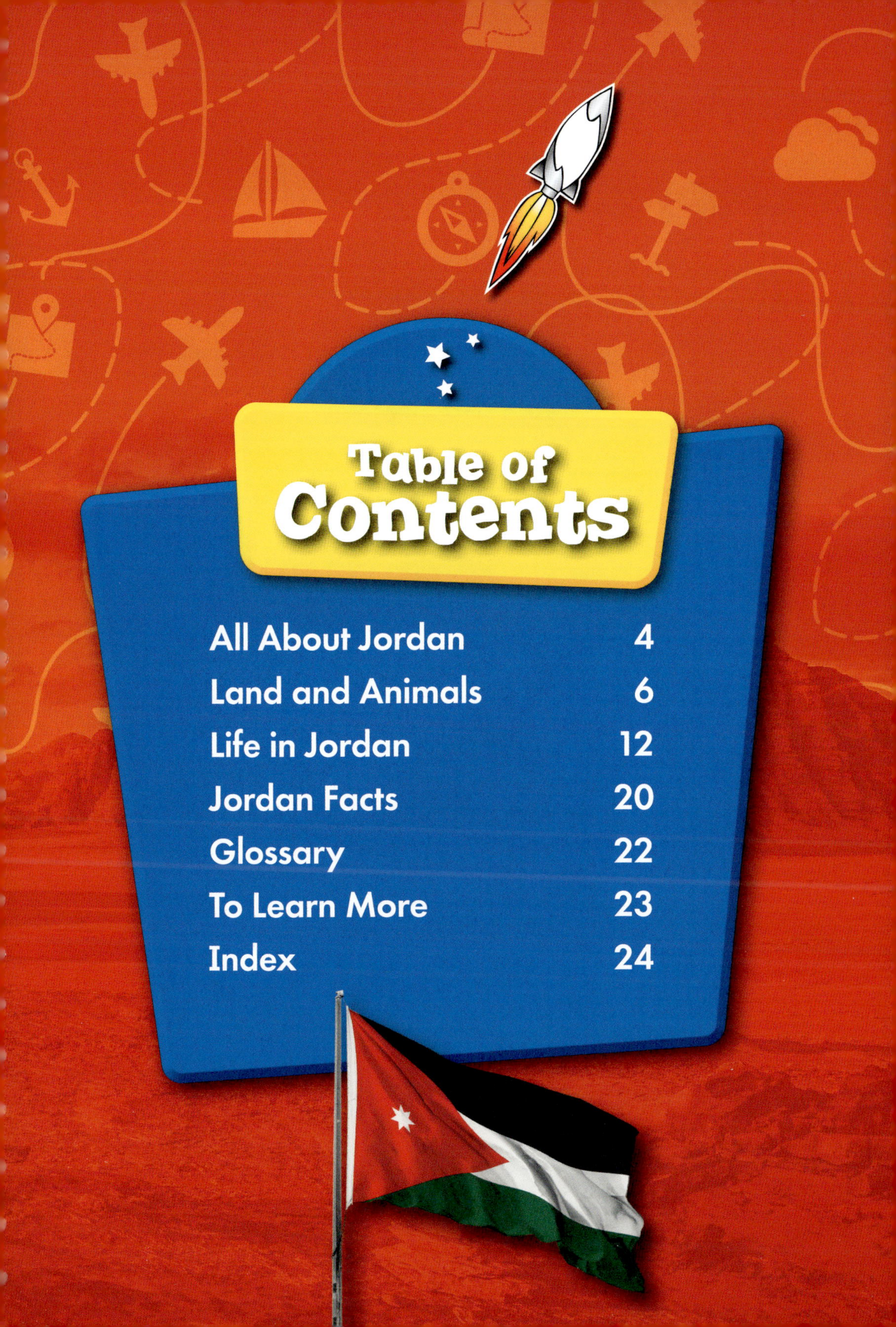

Table of Contents

All About Jordan

Amman

Jordan is a country in Asia.
It is part of the **Middle East**.
Amman is the capital.

Jordan is known for its amazing **archaeological** sites.

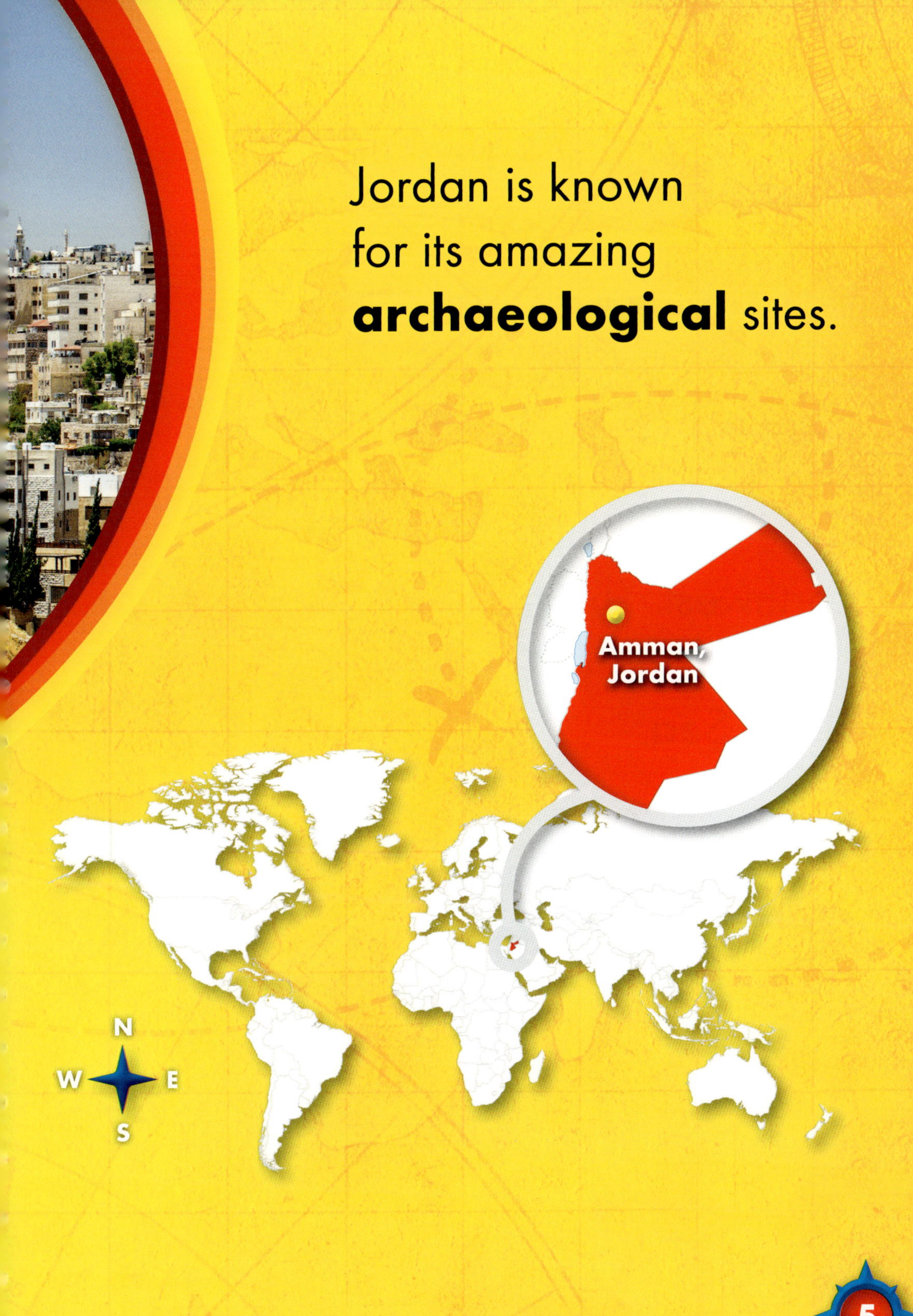

Land and Animals

Desert covers most of Jordan. Mountains rise in the west.

The Jordan Valley is in the northwest. The Jordan River flows through it into the Dead Sea.

desert

The Dead Sea

Deepest Point: 1,083 feet (330 meters)

Famous For: a salt lake that fills the lowest land point on Earth

Jordan is **arid**. Hot winds blow from the southeast during summer.

Winter is cooler with a little rain. Sandstorms blow across the country.

Eagles and other birds **migrate** over Jordan. Ibex climb up rocky mountains.

Scorpions hide under desert rocks. Jackals hunt in the valley.

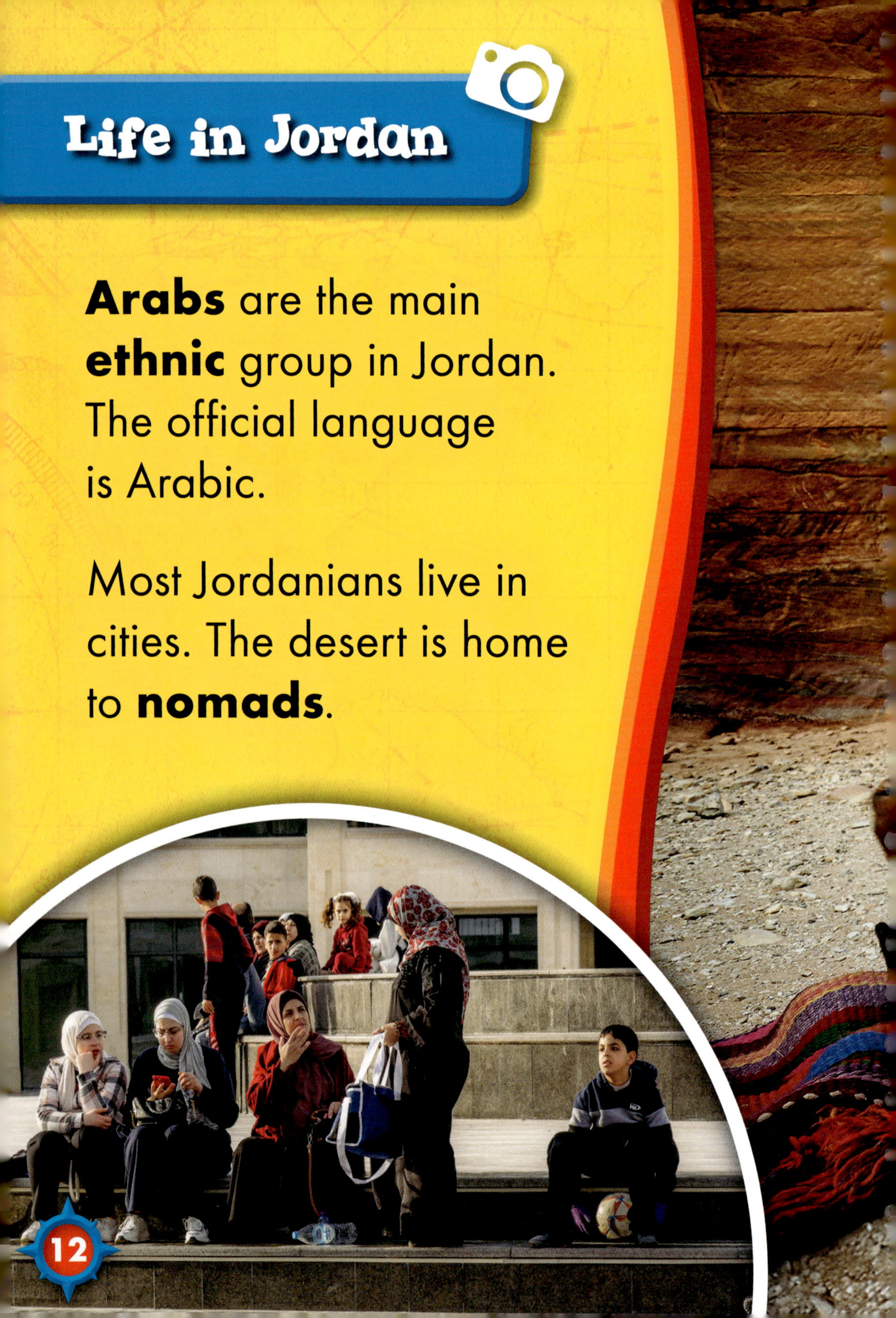

Life in Jordan

Arabs are the main **ethnic** group in Jordan. The official language is Arabic.

Most Jordanians live in cities. The desert is home to **nomads**.

English: Hello
Arabic: Marhaba
(mar-HAB-ah)

Art and music are important parts of Jordan's **culture**. People enjoy dances such as *dabke*. They visit the country's museums.

Soccer and basketball are both popular in Jordan.

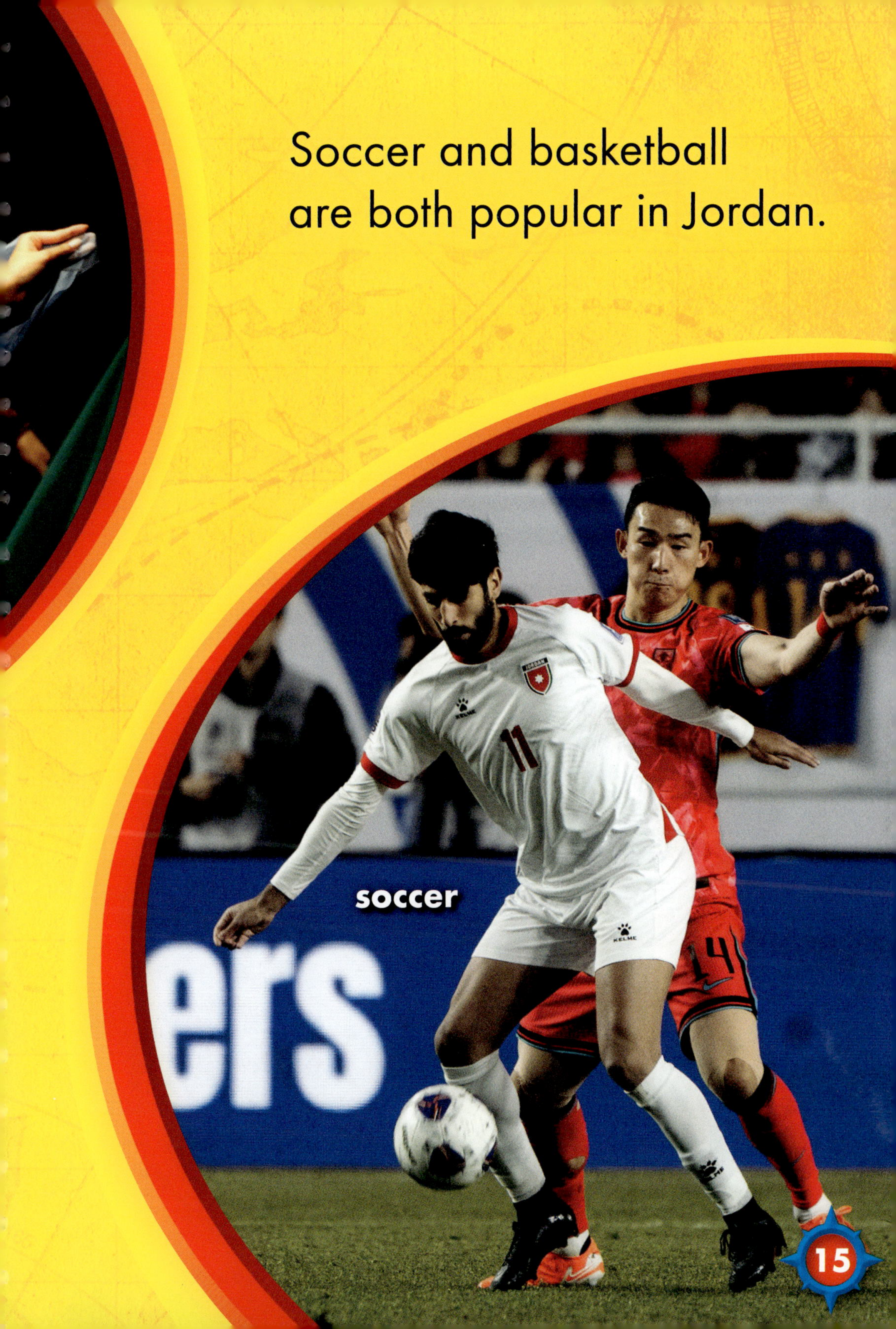

soccer

Mansaf is lamb cooked in yogurt. *Manakish* is flatbread with toppings.

hummus

Falafel and hummus are popular snacks. *Warbat* is a crispy pastry. It is filled with sweet cream!

Ramadan is a monthlong holiday. People pray and **fast**.

The Jerash **Festival** is in summer. It includes concerts and plays. Jordanians are proud of their culture!

Jordan Facts

Size:
34,495 square miles
(89,342 square kilometers)

Population:
11,174,024 (2024)

National Holiday:
Independence Day (May 25)

Main Language:
Arabic

Capital City:
Amman

Famous Face

Name: Ahmad Abughaush

Famous For: taekwondo athlete who won Jordan's first Olympic gold medal

Religions

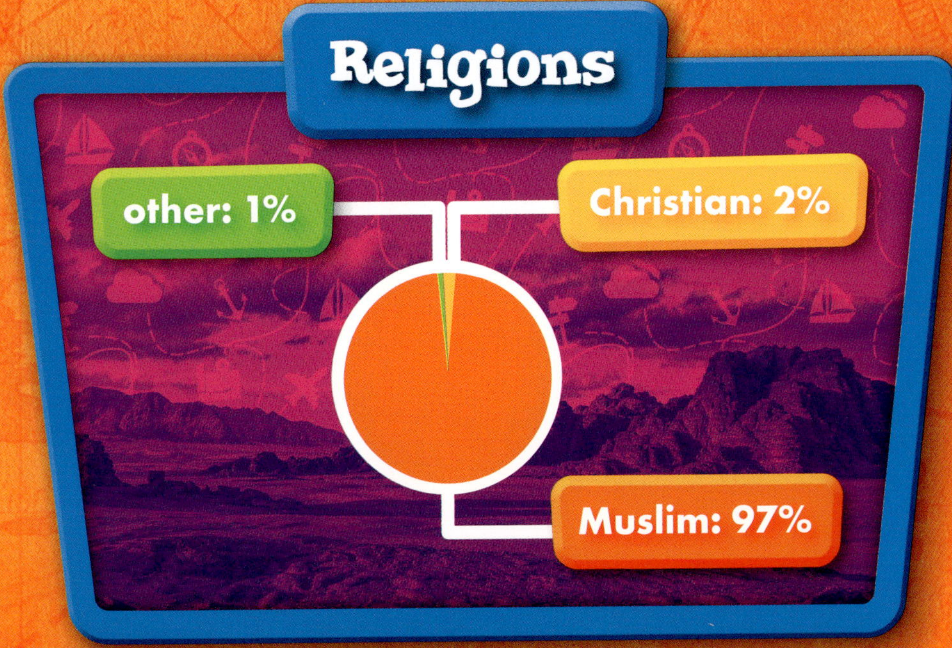

Top Landmarks

Jerash

Petra

Wadi Rum Protected Area

Glossary

Arabs–people who live mostly in the Middle East and northern Africa

archaeological–related to the study of things left behind by ancient people

arid–very dry, with little rainfall

culture–the beliefs, arts, and ways of life in a place or society

desert–an area of dry land with few plants and little rainfall

ethnic–related to races or large groups of people who share things such as customs, religion, and language

fast–to stop eating all or some foods for a certain period of time

festival–a time or event of celebration

Middle East–a region of southwestern Asia and northern Africa; this region includes Egypt, Lebanon, Iran, Iraq, Israel, Saudi Arabia, Syria, and other nearby countries.

migrate–to move from one place to another, often with the seasons

nomads–people who have no fixed home but wander from place to place

To Learn More

AT THE LIBRARY

Darraj, Susan Muaddi. *See and Say Arabic.* North Mankato, Minn.: Pebble, 2025.

Nargi, Lela. *Desert Biomes.* Minneapolis, Minn.: Jump!, 2023.

Quick, Megan. *Do You Dare Visit the Dead Sea?* Buffalo, N.Y.: Enslow Publishing, 2024.

ON THE WEB

FACTSURFER

Factsurfer.com gives you a safe, fun way to find more information.

1. Go to www.factsurfer.com.
2. Enter "Jordan" into the search box and click 🔍.
3. Select your book cover to see a list of related content.

Index

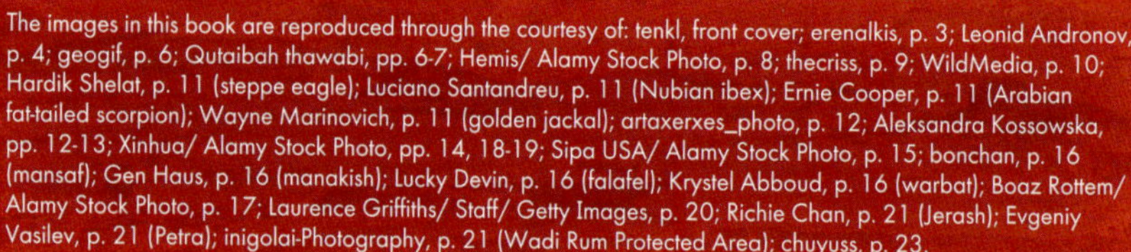

The images in this book are reproduced through the courtesy of: tenkl, front cover; erenalkis, p. 3; Leonid Andronov, p. 4; geogif, p. 6; Qutaibah thawabi, pp. 6-7; Hemis/ Alamy Stock Photo, p. 8; thecriss, p. 9; WildMedia, p. 10; Hardik Shelat, p. 11 (steppe eagle); Luciano Santandreu, p. 11 (Nubian ibex); Ernie Cooper, p. 11 (Arabian fat-tailed scorpion); Wayne Marinovich, p. 11 (golden jackal); artaxerxes_photo, p. 12; Aleksandra Kossowska, pp. 12-13; Xinhua/ Alamy Stock Photo, pp. 14, 18-19; Sipa USA/ Alamy Stock Photo, p. 15; bonchan, p. 16 (mansaf); Gen Haus, p. 16 (manakish); Lucky Devin, p. 16 (falafel); Krystel Abboud, p. 16 (warbat); Boaz Rottem/ Alamy Stock Photo, p. 17; Laurence Griffiths/ Staff/ Getty Images, p. 20; Richie Chan, p. 21 (Jerash); Evgeniy Vasilev, p. 21 (Petra); inigolai-Photography, p. 21 (Wadi Rum Protected Area); chuyuss, p. 23.